# *DIFFICULT LOGIC PUZZLES FOR SMART KIDS*

## *150 BRAINTEASERS AND PUZZLES THE WHOLE FAMILY WILL LOVE*

### *M. PREFONTAINE*

i

# INTRODUCTION

*The mind, once stretched by a new idea, never returns to its original dimensions. Ralph Waldo Emerson (1803 - 82)*

This book is a collection of challenging puzzles which are designed for smart kids of 12+ years, and for the whole family to participate. Indeed, solutions for many puzzles may well need a collaborative effort.

The purpose is to stretch the mind by thinking through puzzles using logic and lateral thinking. Even if you eventually have to look up the answer the fact that the problem has been mentally wrestled with will have stretched the brain. It is the process which is beneficial not the end result.

*The only mistake is one from where we learn nothing. Henry Ford (1863 – 1947)*

The book is laid out in three chapters which get more difficult as you go through the book. The solutions, with explanations, are at the back of the book

This book is part of the Series "Books for Smart Kids". Books in this series include;

Difficult Riddles For Smart Kids

Math Riddles For Smart Kids

Difficult Word Search For Smart Kids

# CONTENTS

Page

# DIFFICULT PUZZLES

## 1. BOY AND A GIRL

A boy and a girl are sat on a park bench.

The blonde-haired child says;
"I am a girl"

The brown-haired child says;
"I am a boy".

Which is the girl, and which is the boy if at least one of them is lying?

## 2. A WINDY DAY

A plane flies regularly between two airports A and B. It flies A to B and then back to A again. The distance is 500 miles each way and the plane flies at 200 miles per hour on a day without wind.

However, on this day the wind is blowing at 50 miles per hour and the plane flies from A to B with the wind and back to A against the wind.

Will the plane be in the air for more time, less time or the same amount of time on the windy day as a day with no wind?

## 3. Day of the week

A logician was asked what day it was today. As always, he couldn't give a simple answer and said; "If yesterday was tomorrow today would be Friday"

What day of the week did he say this on?

## 4. Pocket Money Millionaire

You are given 1p pocket money in the first week and it doubles every week thereafter to 2p in the second week, 4p in the third etc.

How long would it be before you were a millionaire?

## 5. Pills

You have five jars containing pills. Each pill weighs 10g apart from those in a contaminated jar which weigh 9g.

You have a set of scales. How can you tell which jar the contaminated pills are in with one measurement?

## 6. Manhole Covers

An easy one. Why are manhole covers usually round rather than square, rectangular or some other shape?

# 7. THE MURDERER

A murderer is condemned to death. He has to choose between three rooms. The first is full of raging fires, the second is full of assassins with loaded guns, and the third is full of lions that haven't eaten in 3 years.

Which room is safest for him?

# 8. THE SECURITY GUARDS

Two security guards were on duty outside a bank. One faced up the road to watch for anyone approaching from the North. The other looked down the road to see if anyone approached from the South.

Suddenly one of them said to the other, "Why are you smiling?"

How did he know his companion was smiling?

# 9. POP

One supermarket is doing 3 for 2 offers on lemonade, while a rival over the road is doing 30% off.

If you want 3 bottles of lemonade which is cheapest?

# 10. Sock Drawer

In your sock drawer you have 11 blue socks, 12 red socks, 13 pink socks, 14 brown socks and 15 purple socks.

If you take your socks out at random how many do you have to take out to get a matching pair?

# 11. Total Darkness

A completely black dog was strolling down a street during a total blackout which affected the entire town. Not a single streetlight had been on for several hours. As the dog crosses the center of the road a car with 2 broken headlights speeds towards it, but manages to swerve out of the way just in time.

How could the driver see the dog to swerve in time?

# 12. Grandma's Cakes

You are going to take some of the cakes you have baked to your grandma. However, you must cross seven bridges to reach her house, and at each bridge there is a robber.

Each of these robbers demand a half of the cakes that you are carrying, though they will return one of these cakes as they are for your grandma.

How many cakes will you have to leave home with to guarantee that you can give grandma two cakes?

## 13. BALLS AND BOWLS

You have two empty bowls and 50 white balls and 50 black balls. You put all the balls into the two bowls and a ball is picked at random.

How do you distribute the balls between the two bowls to maximize the chances of a white ball being picked?

## 14. CAMELS

You are in a desert and there are several travelers and several camels. The following statements are both true;

a) If each traveler sits on a camel, there is one traveler who doesn't get a camel
b) If two travelers sit on each camel, then one camel doesn't have any travelers.

How many travelers and camels are there?

## 15. ONE TRUTH

There are three statements and only one can be a true.

a) Answer A
b) Answer B or A
c) Answer B or C

Which answer is correct?

## 16. EGGS

Which came first the chicken or the egg?

## 17. THE CUBE

A cube 3" x 3" x 3" is painted red on all the outside surfaces, including the top and bottom.

If the cube is cut into 27 cubes of 1" x 1" x 1", how many of the 1" cubes have any painted surfaces?

## 18. CARD TRICK

You are dealing a hand in a game of bridge. This involves dealing the cards individually in a clockwise fashion to each of the four players till they have 13 cards each.

However, during the deal a discussion of the previous hand blew up, which is common in bridge, and you forget where you have got to in dealing the cards. None of the players can remember either.

How can you resume the deal immediately without counting how many cards each player has?

## 19. FRAUD

A customer went into a shop and bought an item for $100. The customer paid for the item with a $500 note.

The shopkeeper realized he didn't have change for this note so went to the bank and got change for the note. He paid the customer $400 change.

A couple of days later the bank realized the $500 note was a counterfeit and took $500 back from the shopkeeper.

Who gained and who lost in this transaction?

## 20. THE NEWSPAPER

A newspaper is made from 16 large sheets of paper which are folded in half to create 64 pages of news sheet. The first sheet has the pages 1, 2, 63 and 64.

If we pick out page 45 what are the other page numbers on the sheet?

## 21. THE WISE KINGS DAUGHTER

A wise king devised a contest to see who would receive the Princess' hand in marriage. The Princess was put in a 50 feet x 50 feet carpeted room. Each of her four suitors were put in one corner of the room with a small box to stand on. The first one to touch the Princess' hand would be the winner and become the new King.

The rules were the contestants could not walk over the carpet, cross the plane of the carpet, or hang from anything; nor could they use anything but their body and wits (i.e. no magic, telepathy, nor any items such as ladders, block and tackles etc).

One suitor figured out a way and married the Princess and became the new King. What did he do?

## 22. A MUM

Janes mum had four children. The first was called April, the second May and the third June.

What was the fourth child called?

## 23. PREFIX

Which two letters can prefix the following words to make six more words?

one
edge
own
ought
awl
aught

# 24. ANTS

There are three ants which are standing on the three corners of a triangle. They randomly pick a direction to walk along the edge of the triangle.

They continue to walk at a constant identical speed. What is the probability that two ants will collide?

# 25. THREE BOXES

You have three boxes and each box has two balls in them. One has two black balls, one has two white balls and the other has a white and black ball. They are labelled for their contents BB, WW and BW. However, due to a clerical error the labels have been mixed up and they are all incorrectly labelled.

You can draw balls out of the boxes, without seeing the remaining balls. How can you tell the correct contents of each box by taking just one ball from one box?

# 26. COLLIDING MISSILES

There are two missiles that are heading straight for each other. The first missile is traveling at 9,000mph and the second one at 21,000mph.

What is the distance between the missiles one minute before they collide?

## 27. The Trapped Frog

A frog has had the misfortune to fall down a 30 meter well. Every day it can jump 3 meters but slips back by two meters during the night.

If we assume that every 3 meter jump lifts his hind legs 3 meters how long before he can get out of the well?

## 28. Skiing holiday

You are off for a skiing holiday and have invested in some brand new 5ft skis. However, you find out the airline will not allow items 5ft long on board. The maximum size item that it will allow on board is 4ft by 3ft.

How do you get to take your skis on the plane with you?

## 29. School Books

There are three schools who want 1,500 text books between them.

We know that one school wants 10 times as many as another school and another wants 4 times as many as another school.

How many books does each school want?

## 30. Zero to Infinity

If you were to put all the numbers from zero to infinity in alphabetical order what number would come second?

## 31. Cricket

Bob went to the beach to play cricket with his children. On the way he bought a bat and a ball for £11.

The bat cost £10 more than the ball. How much did each cost?

## 32. The Wall

Jack and Bob are both building a wall in their spare time. The walls will require 500 bricks each to be laid.

Jack is laying the bricks so that on the first day he lays one brick, on the second day he lays 2 bricks, on the third day he lays 4 and so on.

Bob lays the bricks differently. He lays 10 bricks on the first day, 20 on the second day, 30 on the third day and so on.

Who completes their wall first?

## 33. Seven Letter Word

Using only the four letters below as often as you want, create a seven letter word;

## 34. BOOMERANG BALL

Jack throws a tennis ball as hard as he can. It doesn't bounce off anything and no one throws it back to him. However, it comes straight back to him.

How does he do that?

## 35. THE GIFT

A benefactor gives a fixed amount of money equally each week to a number of needy people in his neighborhood. If there were five fewer needy people, then the remaining ones would get $2 more.

However, on this day there were four extra people rather than five less. The result was that they each got $1 less.

How much did the needy get in the last distribution?

## 36. THE PUPPY

Jack's new puppy was growing very quickly. Each day it ate 6 more biscuits than the previous day. After 5 days it had eaten 100.

How many did it eat on the first day?

## 37. THE NEW CAR

A new car was reduced in price by 20% in the sale. Once the sale ends how much must the price rise to return to the original price?

## 38. THE CAR JOURNEY

A car travels the first half of its journey at 40mph and the second half at 60mph.

What was its average speed?

## 39. AUGUSTUS DE MORGAN

The famous mathematician, who died in 1871, was fond of saying that he was x years old in the year $x^2$.

When was he born?

## 40. DEMOCHARES

Demochares has lived 1/4 of his life as a boy, 1/5 as a youth, 1/3 as a man and spent 13 years in his dotage.

How old is Demochares?

## 41. FOREST FIRE

Jim is holidaying by himself on an island which is covered in forest. One day there is a very strong wind blowing from the west and lightning strikes the west end and starts a fire.

The fire is very violent and will spread across the whole island and will kill Jim unless something happens.

There are no buckets or extinguishers and sharks are prevalent in the water around the island, so he cannot go in the sea.

How can he survive?

## 42. HOT DOGS

A man and a half can eat a hot dog and a half in a minute and a half.

How long would it take six men to eat six hot dogs?

## 43. THE ARCHBISHOP'S CANDLES

Under financial pressure, the Archbishop decides to save money by recycling candles. One new candle can be formed from ten melted candle stubs.

In total, how many candles can the Archbishop burn from an initial inventory of 2018 candles?

# 44. THE DITCH

Bill and Harry can dig a ditch in twenty four days. If Bill can only do two thirds as much as Harry how long will it take if they do the work alone?

# 45. THE PRINTERS PROBLEM

A printer has 50,000 invoice books to print for each month for a customer during the year. The problem is he must change the month at the top from January to February to March etc.

Print types are very expensive, so he decides to reuse the types from each month once he has printed the 50,000 books for the previous month.

How many separate letter types did he have to purchase to be able to do every month?

# 46. HALLOWEEN

In a particular year there were four Tuesdays and four Fridays in October.

What day of the week was Halloween, October 31st, that year?

# 47. ALPHABETICAL NUMBER

Which number when spelt out is in alphabetical order?

# 48. FILLING THE TANK

We have two separate water pipes A and B, which can feed water at a constant rate into a water tank.

Pipe A alone would fill an empty tank in 1 hour 20 minutes.

Pipe B alone would fill an empty tank in 2 hours.

If both pipes were filling the tank at the same time, how long would it take to fill an empty tank?

# 49. THE FISH

A fish has a tail as long as its head and 1/4 the length of its body. Its body is 3/4 of its total length. Its head is 4 inches long.

How long is the fish?

# 50. HIDDEN INSTRUMENTS

What musical instruments are represented below?

a)  P O
b)  BA BA
c)  ECLART
d)  %$&#

## 51. FUNDRAISING

A stall at a school fair is offering cash in a game to raise funds for the school. It has a bag of six balls, half of which are green and the other half red. For a donation to the school, players draw 3 balls out of the bag at random, sight unseen. For each player who draws all 3 green balls, the stallholder will double their money.

What is the chance of a player winning the cash?

## 52. NUMBERS

What number replaces the question mark in this sequence?

5  9  14  23  ?  60  97

## 53. THE TUNNEL

A 440 yard long train, travelling at 60 mph, enters a one mile long tunnel.

How long will elapse between the moment the front of the train enters the tunnel and the moment the end of the train clears the tunnel?

## 54. A WORD

What word of one syllable becomes a three-syllable word when one more letter is added?

## 55. THE MOST MOVING PARTS

A sundial is a timepiece with the least moving parts. What timepiece has the most moving parts?

## 56. PERSPECTIVE

How do you make the following equation add up without changing it?

8 + 8 = 91

## 57. SUBTRACTION

Subtractus Minimus said he could take one away from 19 and get 20.

How is this possible?

## 58. LETTERS

How many letters are there in the answer to this question?

## 59. HEADING SOUTH

If you happened to live in Atlanta, Georgia, and flew directly south which would be the first South American country you would fly over?

# 60. HAD HAD

Can you put proper grammar into the words below, without changing them or their order, so that it makes sense?

Alex where Paul had had had had had had had had had was the answer

# 61. TENNIS TOURNAMENT

You are organizing a tennis knockout tournament and there are 119 entrants who want to play.

How many matches do you have to arrange to get a winner?

# 62. GOING FOR A RUN

Jack and Harry have the exact same walking speed and the exact same running speed.

One day they started the same trip to the same place. Jack walked for half of the distance and ran the rest while Harry walked for half of the time and ran for the other half of the time.

Who reached the end of the trip first?

# 63. FIVE SISTERS

There are five sisters in a room. They are all occupied.

Margaret is cooking
Kate is playing chess
Ann is reading a book
Marie is doing the laundry

What is the fifth sister doing?

## 64. A BOUQUET OF FLOWERS

In a bouquet of flowers, all but two are roses, all but two are tulips, and all but two are daisies.

How many flowers are in the bouquet?

## 65. ESCAPING THE EXECUTIONER

A prisoner is told "If you tell a lie we will hang you; if you tell the truth we will shoot you."

What can he say to save himself?

## 66. SIBLINGS

Two women go for a job interview. They look identical, have the same birthday as well as the same mother and father.

The interviewer asked if they were twins and they truthfully answered no.

Why are they not twins?

## 67. Exceptional Paragraph

This is an unusual paragraph. I'm curious as to just how quickly you can find out what is so unusual about it. It looks so ordinary and plain that you would think nothing was wrong with it. In fact, nothing is wrong with it. It is highly unusual though. Study it and think about it, but you still may not find anything odd. But if you work at it a bit, you might find out. Why is it unusual?

## 68. Ice Cube

A single ice cube sits in a glass of water on a table. The ice cube gradually melts.

Will the level of the water in the glass have increased, decreased or stay the same?

## 69. A Bus Driver

You are the bus driver. At your first stop, you pick up 29 people. On your second stop, 18 of those 29 people get off, and at the same time 10 new passengers arrive. At your next stop, 3 of those 10 passengers get off, and 13 new passengers come on. On your fourth stop 4 of the remaining 10 passengers get off, 6 of those new 13 passengers get off as well, then 17 new passengers get on.

What is the color of the bus driver's eyes?

# 70. SILLY NUMBERS

Susan gets 10, and Jim and Neal both get 5 but Richard gets 10.

How many does Jennifer get by this system?

# FIENDISH PUZZLES

### 71. BOY OR A GIRL

Bill and Chloe have two children. We know that one of them is a boy. If we assume that the probability of having a boy or a girl is ½ what is the probability that the other child is also a boy?

## 72. SHERLOCK HOLMES

The great detective was investigating a crime. In the following statements only one is true and three are lies;

Abbie: Britney did it
Britney: Abbie did it
Charles: Britney is telling the truth
David: Charles isn't lying

Who did Sherlock say committed the crime?

## 73. TIMING FUSES

You have two identical fuses which will each burn for an hour when lit. However, they do not burn uniformly so that the halves could burn in 10 minutes and 50 minutes for example.

You also have some matches. How can you measure 45 minutes using the fuses and matches?

# 74. MIDAS

Midas employed a gardener for a week. Unfortunately, he only had gold to pay him with. He has a gold rod of 7 units which make 7 days' pay.

He can only make two cuts in this rod. How can he split the rod up so that he can pay him the correct amount every day?

# 75. GOOD JOB DONE

A man is given a job to do. As he is doing the job he gets better and better at it. In fact, he doubles the amount he does every day he does the task.

The task takes 10 days. After how many days has he done 25% of the task?

# 76. OFFSPRING

My eldest daughter has the same number of sisters as she has brothers. However, each of her brothers has twice as many sisters as brothers.

How many sons and daughters do I have?

# 77. THE CAR THIEVES

There were three car thieves Andy, Jack and Liam. They stole three cars – a Jaguar, a Mercedes and a Bentley. Each stole one vehicle.

They made some statements;

Andy: Liam stole the Jaguar

Jack: Liam stole the Mercedes

Liam: I stole neither the Jaguar or the Mercedes.

Police discover that the thief who stole the Jaguar was telling the truth.

Which suspect stole which car?

## 78. RICH AND POOR

There are two types of people the Poor and the Rich. The characteristics of these two people are that the Poor always tell the truth while the Rich always lie.

You have a chat with Fred and Lisa. Fred says, "Lisa is Poor" and Lisa says "The two of us are opposite types"

What types are Fred and Lisa?

## 79. HOUR GLASSES

You have two hour glasses one of which will run for 4 minutes and one of which will run for 7 minutes.

How do you measure 9 minutes using these two hour glasses?

## 80. THE TRAVELER

A man regularly travels to the railway station where his wife picks him up and takes him home. He usually gets the train which gets him to the station for 5pm.

However, on this day he manages to get the earlier train and arrives at the station at 4pm. He decides that he needs the exercise and rather than telephoning his wife begins to walk home.

His wife meets him as he is walking and picks him up and he eventually arrives home 10 minutes earlier than usual.

The wife always drives at a constant speed and had left in time to pick him up at 5pm. How long did he walk for?

## 81. THE PERILOUS ROOM

You are stuck in a room with two doors. One door leads to freedom and the other to certain death. The problem is you don't know which is which.

There are two guards to the doors and you can ask them one question to help you make your mind up. However one of the guards always tells the truth and the other always lies.

What question would you ask to be sure of safety?

## 82. A Pet Pigeon

Two friends decide to meet up. They live 36 miles away from each other and intend to cycle to their meeting point. They can both cycle at 6 mph.

One of the cyclists also has a pet pigeon that he brings along. The pigeon starts flying as soon as they start cycling and flies back and forth between the two friends until they meet up. The pigeon flies at 18mph.

How far does the pigeon fly?

## 83. The Zookeeper

A zookeeper oversaw the feeding of several animals. They were the bears, giraffes, monkeys, lions and zebras.

He fed them in the same order every day. The clues to the order are;

a) The giraffes were fed before the zebras but after the monkeys
b) The bears were fed after the monkeys
c) The lions were fed after the zebras

In what order were the animals fed?

# 84. Burglar Bill

Burglar Bill can carry 52kg in his swag bag. His victim's home has five each of diamonds, sapphires, and rubies.

The diamonds, sapphires, and rubies are worth £23, £36, and £10 respectively, and weigh 7kg, 11kg, and 3kg respectively. How should he fill his bag to extract the maximum the value from his theft?

# 85. A Bag of Spuds

A bag of potatoes weighs 50lbs divided by half its weight.

How much does the bag weigh?

# 86. The Tourists

There was a group of 35 tourists who were being taken around a monument. There are twice as many women as children and twice as many children as men.

How many men, women and children are there in the group?

# 87. The Legacy

A father left $1,000 to his two sons Ian and David. If one third of Ian's legacy is taken from one fourth of David's the amount remaining would be $110.

How much did each of the sons receive?

## 88. JACK AND JEN

If you have Jack's age, square it and add it to Jen's age you get 62. However, if you have Jen's age and square it and add it to Jack's age you get 176.

What ages are Jack and Jen?

## 89. BILL'S PAINTERS

Bill hired two painters to paint two rooms in his house and it took them two hours. He liked it so much that he wanted the other 18 rooms in his house done in 6 hours.

How many painters would he need?

## 90. A NUMBER

What number is 3 times the sum of its digits?

## 91. HARROD'S

100 women were observed leaving Harrod's. 83 had a white bag, 77 had black shoes, 62 were carrying an umbrella and 95 were wearing a ring.

What is the minimum number of women who must have had all four items?

# 92. ANN'S AGE

Ann was trying to remember how old she was. She said "My brother is two years older than me, and my sister is four years older than him. My mother's age was twenty when I was born"

The average age of the four of them is 39. What is Ann's age?

# 93. THE MATHEMATICIAN

A farmer challenges an engineer, a physicist, and a mathematician to fence off the largest amount of area using the least amount of fencing.

The engineer designed his fence in a circle and said it was the most efficient way to fence an area.

The physicist made a line and said that the length was infinite. Then he said that fencing half of the Earth was the best.

The mathematician laughed at the others and with his design, beat the others. What did he do?

# 94. CLOCK FACE

How many degrees are there between the hands of a clock at quarter past three?

## 95. THE WINDY DOG

A dog can run a mile in 3 minutes with the wind behind it. However, the return journey against the wind takes 4 minutes.

How long would it take to run a mile without any wind?

## 96. PILL TAKING

Jeff needs to take an antibiotic four times a day, at equally-spaced intervals. He takes his first pill at 6am and his last pill at 10pm.

How long should he wait between taking successive pills?

## 97. FRIENDS AGE

A friend tells you that they are 35 if you don't count Saturdays or Sundays.

How old are they?

## 98. A CHILD

Ann is 21 years older than her child. In precisely 6 years from now Ann will be precisely 5 times older than her child.

How old is the child now?

## 99. MINCE PIES

A bakery has prepared some mince pies. The first customer to the store purchases three quarters of the pies for a Christmas party that evening. The second customer takes half of the remaining, then buys seven more for a friend. The third customer takes the last 9 of the batch.

How many were there to start with?

## 100. SUGAR AND SPICE

Who on average has more sisters, girls or boys?

## 101. A LONG PIECE OF STRING

You have a long piece of string which you put tightly around the earth at the equator. That makes it about 40,000,000 meters in length. We are assuming that the earth is a perfect sphere.

Now you increase the length of string by 10 meters uniformly around the earth so that it is suspended over the surface equally.

What is the gap between the surface of the earth and the string?

# 102. THE NECKTIE PARADOX

Two men are each given a necktie by their respective wives as a present. Over drinks they start arguing over who has the more expensive necktie and agree to have a bet. They will ask their wives and find out which necktie is the more expensive. The man with the more expensive necktie has to give it to the other as the prize.

The first man reasons as follows: the probability of me winning or losing is 50:50. If I lose, then I lose the value of my necktie. If I win, then I win more than the value of my necktie. In other words, I can bet x and have a 50% chance of winning more than x. Therefore, it is in my interest to make the bet.

The second man can consider the bet in exactly the same way; therefore, paradoxically, it seems both men have the advantage in taking the bet.

How can both men have the advantage in the bet?

# 103. POOL PARTY COKE

You are with some friends at a pool party. Somebody brings a cooler which is filled with Coke and Diet Coke. You're diabetic, so you open the cooler to grab a Diet Coke when you discover that someone has taken the labels off all the bottles.

Both are in identical plastic bottles, and as best as you can determine, the cola inside both looks identical in every way.

Without opening any of the bottles, how can you determine which bottles are filled with Diet Coke?

## 104. SOLVE THE SUM

Can you solve the following addition where A, B and C represent different digits?

```
  A B C
  A B C
  A B C
  C C C
```

## 105. HOUSE HUNTING

While house hunting I come across a very pleasant flat. The owner tells me that the property was originally on a 99 years lease. However today two-thirds of the time passed is equal to four-fifths of the time to come.

How long is left on the lease?

## 106. WEIGHTS

What are the four different weights that can be used to on a set of scales to enable between 1 and 30 pounds to be weighed?

## 107. THE MARKSMAN

A marksman puts two bullets into a six-chamber revolver. He puts the bullets into consecutive chambers and gives the barrel a spin.

He then fires the gun and it is a blank.

Are the odds greater of him actually firing a bullet if he spins the chamber again or just fires the gun without spinning?

## 108. ST IVES

On my way to St Ives I saw a man with seven wives, each wife had seven children and each child had seven pet cats.

How many were going to St Ives?

## 109. IN THE DARK

One night, Uncle Tom and Auntie Jane were in the living room reading books. Tom said he was going to bed and turned the light off.

Auntie Jane carried on reading. How was this?

# 110. Poultry Puzzle

Three chickens and one duck sold for as much as two geese; one chicken, two ducks, and three geese were sold together for $25.00.

What was the price of each bird in an exact number of dollars?

# Evil Puzzles

## 111. The Bridge

Adam, Betty, Chris and Diane were crossing a rickety bridge at night. Only two people could cross at a time and due to the state of the bridge they had to have a torch. They had a torch, but it only had 15 minutes of battery left.

The speed they could each cross the bridge was;
Adam – 1 minute
Betty – 2 minutes
Chris – 5 minutes
Diane – 8 minutes

If two go together they go at the speed of the slowest.

Can they all cross the bridge before the torch battery expires?

## 112. The Missing Dollar

Three guests check into a hotel for a room for the night. The manager tells them the room is $30. He later realizes that he should have charged them $25 so he gives the bellhop $5 and tells him to return it to the guests.

The bellhop realizes that he can't split the $5 between the three guests so he gives them $1 each and keeps $2 as a tip for himself.

The net effect of this is that each guest paid $9 which adds up to $27. If we include the $2 the bellhop received it adds up to $29.

So, what has happened to the missing dollar from the $30 they originally paid?

## 113. LOVING AND GIVING

A mother had five boys: Michael, Thomas, William and Timothy.

Was the fifth boys name Alex, James or Frank?

## 114. THE CENSUS

A census was being taken and the census taker came upon a woman in her garden and asks her how many children she has.

She says that she has three children and if you multiply their ages together you get 72, and if you add their ages together you get the number on the gate of the house.

The census taker has a think and tells the woman that he needs more information. The woman says she hasn't got the time as her eldest child was ill in bed.

From this the census taker was satisfied. What were the children's ages?

## 115. THE MONTY HALL PROBLEM

You find yourself on a game show. The host offers you three doors. Behind one door is a brand new Ferrari and behind the other two there is nothing.

You pick door number 1. The host, who knows what is behind the doors then opens one of the other doors, as with every contestant, and there is nothing behind it.

He then asks if you want to switch from door number 1 or pick the other unopened door.

Do you switch doors?

## 116. CAMELS AND BANANAS

You have 3,000 bananas that you want transporting 1,000 miles across the desert. You also have a camel to transport them. However, this camel can only carry 1,000 bananas at a time and eats 1 banana for every mile it travels.

You can load and unload as many bananas as you want anywhere. What is the most bananas you can get to the destination 1,000 miles away?

# 117. Card Trick

You are presented with the four cards each card has a number on one side and a letter on the other. You can only see one side face up.

You are told that every card that has a vowel on one side has an even number on its opposite side.

The first card has an E, the second a G, the third a 2 and the fourth a 3.

Which cards must you turn over to ascertain the statement true?

# 118. Cheryl's Birthday

Cheryl's birthday is on one of the following dates;

May: 15th, 16th or 19th
June: 17th or 18th
July: 14th or 16th
August:14th, 15th or 17th

She was a bit coy about her birthday but did tell Albert the month and Bernard the day.

Albert and Bernard then discussed the matter:

Albert: I don't know when Cheryl's birthday is, but I know Bernard doesn't either.

Bernard: Then I know when Cheryl's birthday is.

Albert: Then I also know when Cheryl's birthday is.

When is Cheryl's birthday?

## 119. Elephants

A King died and left his herd of elephants to his three sons. The first son was to get ½ of the elephants, the second son ¾ of the remaining elephants and his third son ½ of the remaining elephants. There are to be no shared elephants.

The problem is that there are 15 elephants in the herd. How can they be divided without leaving any behind?

## 120. Two Boats

There are two boats, A and B, sailing across a river and start at the same time and at right angles. They travel at constant speeds though one is slightly faster than the other.

They cross each other when A is 720 yards from the nearest shore. Once they reach their intended shore they turn around and return. On their return trip they cross each other when A is 400 yards from the other shore.

How wide is the river?

# 121. A Light Bulb

A room has one wall light, one door and no windows. You cannot see into the room to see if the light is on or off.

Next to the door there are three switches, one of which turns the wall light on and off.

You can turn flick the switches on and off as often as you wish but can only open the door once to check whether the light is on or off.

How do you discover which switch turns the light on?

# 122. The True Statement

There is a list of ten statements. Here are the statements:

In this list, exactly 1 statement is false.
In this list, exactly 2 statements are false.
In this list, exactly 3 statements are false.
In this list, exactly 4 statements are false.
In this list, exactly 5 statements are false.
In this list, exactly 6 statements are false.
In this list, exactly 7 statements are false.
In this list, exactly 8 statements are false.
In this list, exactly 9 statements are false.
In this list, exactly 10 statements are false.

Which of these statements, if any, are logically true?

## 123. A Railway Journey

A railway enthusiast decides to take a trip along a particularly scenic route with 10 beautiful railway stations along it, and back again along the same route.

He takes one photo at each of the stations either on the way out or on the journey back. How many different orders are there in which the photos could have been taken?

## 124. Dates

The date is frequently written as DD/MM/YYYY in which DD is the date, MM is the month and YYYY is the year.

When is the next date that all these numbers will be different?

## 125. Bank Account

You go to your bank to withdraw £100. Your bank informs you that the money that is left in your account has doubled.

How much is left in your account?

# 126. How Old

Alex is twice as old as Tim was when Alex was as old as Tim is now. The combined age of Alex and Tim is 112 years.

How old are Alex and Tim now?

# 127. Which Letter

Which letter comes two to the right of the letter which is immediately to the left of the letter that comes three to the right of the letter that comes midway between the letter two to the left of the letter C and the letter immediately to the right of the letter F?

# 128. Socks

A blind man is searching through his sock drawer for a pair of socks. In his drawer he had only black and white socks and took out two.

His chances of pulling out a pair of white socks was ½. What were the chances of taking out a pair of black socks?

# 129. Bags of Money

A man has $1,000 and 10 bags to put the money in. What amounts must he put into each bag to be able to pay any whole dollar amount, up to $1,000, by handing over one or more bags?

# 130. A WILL

A man left $1,000 in his will to three friends and their wives.

The wives received altogether $396. Jane received $10 more than Catherine, and Mary received $10 more than Jane.

John Smith was given the same amount as his wife, Henry Jones got half as much again as his wife, and Tom White received twice as much as his wife.

What was the Christian name of each man's wife?

# 131. CUBES AND SQUARES

There are two whole numbers whose difference of their squares is a cubic number and the difference of their cubes is a square.

What are the smallest two numbers which fulfill this condition?

# 132. THE OLYMPICS

If FT = GD and SD = SR what does TD equal?

# 133. VEXILLOLOGY

1 = Vietnam
2 = Panama

3 = Burundi
4 = New Zealand
5 = People's Republic of China

What is 6?

## 134. THE DODGY CLOCK

A clock was correct at midnight. From that moment it began to lose four minutes every hour. The clock stopped 90 minutes ago showing 15:52.

The clock runs for less than 24 hours. What is the correct time?

## 135. THE SHOELACE

You are late for a flight. Your journey at the airport involves walking on a travellator and on non-moving ground.

You notice your shoelace is untied and you need to stop to tie it.

Should you tie your shoelace when you're on the travellator or when you're off it to make the most progress, or doesn't it matter?

## 136. TRIPLES

If 125207 is "Hi", and 031993121212 is "Dude", then 125207031993121212 is "Hi Dude".

Then what is
79971777701090923015169312200 1983?

## 137. P<small>LANE</small> S<small>EATING</small>

Jane was the first to board to her flight. She forgot her seat number and picks a random seat for herself.

After this, every single person who gets on the flight sits on his seat if its available or else chooses any available seat at random.

Jack is the last to enter the flight and at that moment 99/100 seats were occupied.

What is the probability that Jack gets to sit in his own seat?

## 138. T<small>WELVE</small> D<small>AYS OF</small> C<small>HRISTMAS</small>

My love gives me gifts as in the 'twelve days of Christmas'. I decide to give them away at a rate of one per day.

If I start on Christmas Day will I have any left to give away on the following Christmas Day?

## 139. A<small>N</small> A<small>THLETIC</small> M<small>IND</small>

What comes next in the sequence?

1, 2, 4, 8, 15 and 50

## 140. ANIMAL ENCYCLOPEDIA

I have an encyclopedia of animals on my shelf, which comes in two volumes. On the left is the Aardvark to Lynx volume, and next to it on the right is the volume for Mackerel to Zebra. Each volume is 5cm thick and the covers are 2mm thick. I have bookmarked two pages, Aardvark and Zebra.

How far apart would you say the two bookmarks are, to the nearest centimeter?

## 141. THE QUEEN OF HEARTS

The Queen of Hearts has lost her tarts. She is certain that those knaves who have not eaten the tarts will tell her the truth and the guilty knave or knaves will tell lies. When questioned the five knaves declare:

Knave 1: 'One of us ate them'
Knave 2: 'Two of us ate them'
Knave 3: 'Three of us ate them'
Knave 4: 'Four of us ate them'
Knave 5: 'Five of us ate them'

How many of the knaves were honest?

# 142. FOOTBALL SCAM

Jane received an email from an unknown source which said that the Crystal Palace would beat Liverpool next Saturday. This seemed unlikely, but it turned out to be correct.

Then the following week she received another email which said Swansea would draw with Manchester United the following Saturday. This also turned out to be correct.

In the five following weeks she received five more forecasts of a win, lose or draw which all turned out to be correct.

Having seen these results she wished that she had put some money on the results.

She then received an email which said if she sent £1,000 she would receive ten correct predictions on which she could put another £1,000 and retire early.

Jane was a bright girl and thought about it and realized it was a scam.

How did they manage to make the correct predictions in the scam?

## 143. The St Petersburg Paradox

A casino is offering you a game with a pot which starts at $1. A fair coin is tossed and if it comes up heads the pot is doubled. However, if it comes up tails you win whatever is in the pot.

The casino is offering to let you play this game for $25. Do you take the offer?

## 144. Four Fours

Use exactly four 4's to form every integer from 0 to 25, using only the operators +, -, x, /, () (brackets), (squared), and ! (factorial).

4! = 4 x 3 x 2 x 1 = 24

## 145. Sixteen Fours

Another question about fours while we have it on the brain.

How can we make 16 fours add up to 1,000?

## 146. A Peculiar Liar

Zac was a peculiar liar.

He lies on six days of the week, but on the seventh day he always tells the truth.

He made the following statements on three successive days:

Day 1: "I lie on Monday and Tuesday."

Day 2: "Today, it is Thursday, Saturday, or Sunday."

Day 3: "I lie on Wednesday and Friday."

On which day does Zac tell the truth?

# 147. DRUGS TEST

Suppose a drug test is 99% sensitive and 99% specific. That is, the test will produce 99% true positive results for drug users and 99% true negative results for non-drug users.

If a randomly selected individual from 1,000 tests turns out to be positive, what is the probability he or she is a user?

# 148. A SOUND RIDDLE

Can you work out the logic behind the following sequence of words?

Gun, shoe, free, door, jive, picks, heaven, gate, pine, when

# 149. Einstein's Puzzle

Einstein said that only 2% of the world could solve this problem.

There are 5 houses in 5 different colors. In each house lives a person with a different nationality. The 5 owners drink a certain type of beverage, smoke a certain brand of cigar, and keep a certain pet. No owners have the same pet, smoke the same brand of cigar, or drink the same beverage.

Clues:
    The Brit lives in the red house.
    The Swede keeps dogs as pets.
    The Dane drinks tea.
    The green house is on the left of the white house.
    The green homeowner drinks coffee.
    The person who smokes Pall Mall rears birds.
    The owner of the yellow house smokes Dunhill.
    The man living in the center house drinks milk.
    The Norwegian lives in the first house.
    The man who smokes Blend lives next to the one who keeps cats.
    The man who keeps the horse lives next to the man who smokes Dunhill.
    The owner who smokes Bluemaster drinks beer.
    The German smokes prince.
    The Norwegian lives next to the blue house.
    The man who smokes Blend has a neighbor who drinks water.

Who owns the fish?

## 150. PRISONER'S TREES

James and Carly are in separate prison cells. From their cells James can see 12 trees and Carly can see 8. They are both told that together they can see all the trees, but that no tree can be seen by both.

Every day the jailor comes to James and asks if there are 18 or 20 trees in total. If he passes he goes and asks Carly the same question. If they both pass, then he comes back the next day and the process repeats.

If either of them gives an incorrect answer then they are kept in prison forever, and if either answer correctly they are freed.

James and Carly cannot communicate with each other. How can they escape without guessing?

# DIFFICULT ANSWERS

### 1. *Boy and a girl*

*An easy one to start with. Both children are lying if at least one of them is as we know that there is a boy and girl on the bench.*

*Therefore, the blonde-haired child is a boy and the brown-haired child is a girl.*

### 2. *A Windy Day*

*Any wind causes the plane to spend more time in the air. Without any wind the 1,000 mile round trip at 200mph will take 5 hours.*

*However, with 50mph wind behind the trip from A to B the plane will be travelling at 250mph and do the 500 miles in 2 hours.*

*The trip from B to A though will be done at 150mph, because of the headwind, which means it will take 3.33 hours to do the 500 miles.*

*The total time with a 50mph wind is therefore 5.33 hours.*

### 3. *Day of the Week*

*It is Wednesday*

## 4. _Pocket Money Millionaire_

_Surprisingly enough it would only take 27 weeks._

_After 10 weeks you will receive £5.12 in the week, but by the 26th week you will get £335,544.32, and by the 27th week £671,088.64. You will therefore have accumulated more than £1 million by 27 weeks._

_You can calculate it on a calculator multiplying 1p by 2 a total of 27 times._

## 5. _Pills_

_You take one pill from jar one, two pills from jar two, three pills from jar three, four pills from jar four and five pills from jar five._

_If the pills were all OK the 15 pills would add up to 150g. However, if the actual weight is 149g then jar one has the contaminated pills, 148 then jar two has the contaminated pills...and so on_

## 6. _Manhole Covers_

_So that the cover can't fall down the hole._

## 7. _The Murderer_

_The last one as the lions would have starved to death._

## 8. _The Security Guards_

_Because they were facing each other_

9. **_Pop_**

If the bottles cost $1 each then the 3 for 2 offer would cost $2.

The full cost of 3 bottles would be $3 and therefore 30% off would be $2.10.

It is best to buy the 3 for 2.

10. **_Sock Drawer_**

There are five distinct colors so if you take out six you will get a matching pair.

11. **_Total Darkness_**

It was daylight

12. **_Grandma's Cakes_**

You need to start with two cakes. You will give one to each robber and then they give you it back to you guaranteeing two cakes for Grandma.

13. **_Balls and Bowls_**

You put one white ball into one bowl and the rest of the balls into the other.

This means that the chances of picking a white ball are $\frac{1}{2}$ + $\frac{1}{2}$ x 49/99 which is approximately a 75% chance of picking a white ball

## 14. _Camels_

_There are 4 travelers and 3 camels_

## 15. _One Truth_

_If the answer were answer a) was correct then that would also mean that answer b) was also correct. This would violate the rule that only one can be correct._

_Similarly, if answer b) were correct then answer c) would also be correct_

_The answer is c)_

## 16. _Eggs_

_The egg. Dinosaurs laid eggs a long time before chickens were around._

## 17. _The Cube_

_All the cubes will have some paint on them apart from the one in the middle. Therefore 26 of the 27 cubes will have paint on a surface._

## 18. _Card Trick_

_You start dealing from the bottom of the pack and give yourself the first card and go around in an anti-clockwise fashion._

## 19. _Fraud_

_The bank didn't lose anything as it got its money back._

*The customer gained the item, worth $100, and the $400 in change he got from the shopkeeper.*

*The shopkeeper lost what the customer gained*

20. **The Newspaper**
*On the back of page 45 is page 46.*

*The numbers are arranged in pairs and the first pair add up to 64 and the second pair add up to 66.*
*Therefore;*
*63+1 = 64*
*64+2 = 66*

*Then;*
*64-45=19*
*66-46=20*

*Therefore, the four pages are 19, 20, 45 and 46*

21. **The Wise Kings Daughter**
*He asked the Princess to come to him and touch his hand*

22. **A Mum**
*Her fourth child was Jane*

23. **Prefix**
*The letters are D & R so we get drone, dredge, drown, drought, drawl and draught*

## 24. __Ants__

The first ant will decide to go clockwise or anti-clockwise. To not collide the other two ants will need to go in the same direction as the first ant.

Whichever direction the first ant goes the chance that other two will go the same way is $1/2 \times 1/2 = 1/4$. Therefore, the chances of a collision are $3/4$.

## 25. __Three Boxes__

We know that the labels are all wrong. If you draw a ball from the box marked BW then whatever color is drawn will be the color of the other ball in this box.

You then have two remaining boxes marked WW and BB. If you drew a black ball from the first box, then you know that WW is wrong and must contain a black and white ball. This leaves BB to contain the two white balls.

## 26. __Colliding Missiles__

500 miles

The missiles are traveling at a combined speed of 30,000mph. They will therefore travel 500 miles in the minute before they collide.

## 27. *The Trapped Frog*

Every day the frog will make up 1 meter. He will make 27 meters on the first 27 days and then jump clear on the 28th.

## 28. *Skiing Holiday*

You get a 4ft by 3ft box and lay the skis across the diagonal. Thank goodness for Pythagoras

## 29. *School Books*

The quantities of books for each school is;

1000, 400 and 100

## 30. *Zero to Infinity*

Eight would be first and eight billion second

## 31. *Cricket*

If you said that the ball cost £1 then you would be wrong as that would mean the bat alone cost £11.

The correct answer is £10.50 and 50p

## 32. *The Wall*

After 8 days Jack will have laid 255 bricks –
1+2+4+8+16+32+64+128

Bob will have laid 360 bricks –
10+20+30+40+50+60+70+80

*On the 9ᵗʰ day Jack would lay 256 bricks taking him over the 500 required for the wall. Meanwhile Bob would lay 90 so he would require an additional day to complete it.*

### 33. <u>**Seven Letter Wall**</u>
*Minimum*

### 34. <u>**Boomerang Ball**</u>
*He throws it straight up in the air. Gravity does the rest*

### 35. <u>**The Gift**</u>
*To begin with there are 20 people and they each receive $6 from the $120 total gift.*

*If there are five fewer applicants, then the 15 will receive $8 each. However, four more will make 24 applicants who receive $5 each*

### 36. <u>**The Puppy**</u>
*The puppy got 8 biscuits on the first day*

### 37. <u>**The New Car**</u>
*If you said 20% you would be wrong. It is 25%*

*If the price was $10,000 and reduced 20% then the price would be $8,000. However, when the price returns to $10,000 it is a 25% increase.*

## 38. *The Car Journey*

*If you said 50mph you are also wrong.*

*Let's take a total distance of 120 miles. At 40mph for half the journey would take 1.5 hours to cover the 60 miles.*

*To cover the 60 miles in the second half of the journey would take 1 hour at 60mph.*

*Therefore the 120 mile journey has taken 2.5 hours and the average speed is 48mph.*

## 39. *Augustus de Morgan*

*He was born in 1806. He was 43 in 1849, which is the square of 43.*

## 40. *Demochares*

*He is 60 years old*

*If Demochares age is x then;*

*$1/3x + 1/4x + 1/5x + 13 = x$*

*$15/60x + 12/60x + 20/60x + 13 = x$*

*$47/60x + 13 = x$*

*$13 = x - 47/60x$ (subtract 47/60x from both sides)*

*13/60x = 13*

*13 x 60/13 = x = 60*

41. **<u>Forest Fire</u>**

   *Jim gets a piece of wood and lights it from the fire on the west end of the island. He takes this to the eastern end of the island and starts a fire.*

   *This will then burn out the eastern end and he can shelter there while the fire from the west burns itself out.*

42. **<u>Hot Dogs</u>**

   *A minute and a half*

   *1.5 men eat 1.5 hotdogs in 1.5mins*
   *Therefore;*
   *1 man eats 1 hotdog in 1.5 mins*
   *Therefore;*
   *6 men eat 6 hotdogs in 1.5mins*

43. **<u>The Archbishop's Candles</u>**

   *The Archbishop starts with 2018 candles and this will create 2018 stubs.*

   *From 2018 stubs we get 201 candles and 8 stubs*

   *From this we get 209 stubs which will create a further 20 candles and 9 stubs.*

From this we get 29 stubs which creates 2 candles with 9 stubs left over. The 2 stubs from the candles and 9 stubs left over will create another candle.

Therefore, the number of candles we have are;

2018
201
20
2
1

The total number of candles is 2,242

## 44. <u>**The Ditch**</u>
If Bill does 2/3 of Harry's work, then Bill will do 40% and Harry 60%.

Therefore, to work out how long it would take Bill is;
100/40 x 24 days = 60 days

Similarly, for Harry it is;

100/60 x 24 = 40 days

## 45. <u>**The Printers Problem**</u>
He needed 27;

AABCDEEEFGHIJLMNOOPRRSTUUVY

## 46. **_Halloween_**
Halloween was on a Monday

## 47. **_Alphabetical Number_**
Forty is the only number in alphabetical order.

## 48. **_Filling the Tank_**
If we assume a tank of 100 gallons then for pipe A to fill it in 1 hour 20 mins would mean water was pouring at 75 gallons an hour.

Similarly, for pipe B to fill it in 2 hours would mean that water was pouring at 50 gallons an hour.

The combined flow of 125 gallons would therefore fill the 100 gallon tank in 48 minutes.

## 49. **_The Fish_**
128 inches
head = 4 inches
body = 96 inches
tail = 28 inches

## 50. **_Hidden Instruments_**
a) Piano (PandO)
b) Tuba (two Bas)
c) Clarinet (Clar in ET
d) Cymbals (symbols)

### 51. *Fundraising*
*The odds are 3/6 x 2/5 x 1/4 which is 1/20*

### 52. **Numbers**
*The number is 37. You need to add the previous two numbers together to get the following number.*

### 53. **The Tunnel**
*1 minute and 15 sec.*

*The train is 0.25-mile-long and traveling 60 miles per hour.*
*Therefore, the front of the train will take 1 min to reach to the end of the tunnel. The body of the train is 1/4 mile and it will take another 15 seconds to clear the tunnel.*

### 54. **A Word**
*The first word is 'are' and if you add another a it becomes 'area'.*

### 55. **The Most Moving Parts**
*An hourglass*

### 56. **Perspective**
*Look at it upside down*

### 57. **Subtraction**
*It is possible if you are a Roman.*

*19 is expressed XIX in Roman numerals. If you take away I you get XX, which is 20.*

## 58. *Letters*

*The answer is four as it is the only number with the same amount of letters as the number.*

## 59. *Heading South*

*If you head south from Atlanta you will miss South America on the western side.*

## 60. *Had Had*

*Alex, where Paul, had had "had", had had "had had". Had had was the answer.*

## 61. *Tennis Tournament*

*118 matches. This is because every player loses once, except for the winner.*

## 62. *Going for a Run*

*Jack runs for half of the distance, so he must be running for less than half of the time. This is because Jack also walks half the distance, and walking the same distance takes more time than running.*

*Since Harry runs half the time, he is running for more time–and walking for less time.*

*Harry will be faster and complete the journey first.*

### 63. *Five Sisters*
*She is playing chess with Kate.*

### 64. *A Bouquet of Flowers*
*There are three flowers. There is 1 rose, 1 tulip and 1 daisy*

### 65. *Escaping the Executioner*
*He can say 'You will hang me'.*

*If they hang him then he was telling the truth and they should shoot him, and vice versa if they shoot him.*

### 66. *Siblings*
*They are part of triplets*

### 67. *Exceptional Paragraph*
*E is the most prolific letter in the English language, but none feature in the paragraph.*

### 68. *Ice Cube*
*The water level stays the same because the ice cube displaces its own weight. This is Archimedes principle.*

### 69. *Bus Driver*
*The question says, 'you are a bus driver'. So, the color of the eyes will be whatever the readers eyes are.*

70. **_Silly Numbers_**

The system is 5 points for every syllable in the word.
Jennifer is therefore 15 points

# FIENDISH ANSWERS

### 71. _**Boy or Girl**_
_The answer surprisingly is 2/3._

_The possibilities for the two children are;_
_Boy – girl_
_Girl – Boy_
_Boy – Boy_
_Girl – Girl_

_We know that girl – girl isn't possible as one of the children is a boy. This leaves three possibilities, two of which are boys. Therefore, the chances are two out of three._

### 72. **Sherlock Holmes**
_Britney did it_

_If Britney did it, then the first statement is true and the other three are false._

_If Abbie did it then Britney's and Charles' statement are true. Remember only one statement can be true_

_If Charles or David did it then all the statements are false_

73. **_Timing Fuses_**

Light up three of the ends of the fuses. When the fuse with two ends lit burns out half an hour will have gone and you light the fourth end.

This second fuse will then take a further 15 minutes before it is burnt out at which time 45 minutes will have elapsed.

74. **_Midas_**

Midas cuts the rod into 3 sections of 1 ,2 and 4 units. He then pays the gardener in the following fashion;

Day 1; he pays him the 1 unit he has cut
Day 2: he pays him the 2 unit piece and takes back the 1 unit
Day 3: gives him the 1 unit to add to the 2 unit he has
Day 4: takes back the 1 and 2 unit and gives him the 4 unit
Day 5: gives back the 1 unit to the gardener
Day 6: takes back the 1 unit and gives him the 2 unit
Day 7: gives him the 1 unit back again

75. **_Good Job Done_**

100% of the task takes 10 days.

So, after 9 days he has done 50% and after 8 days he has done 25% of the task

### 76. _**Offspring**_

*I have four daughters and three sons. Each of my daughters has 3 sisters and 3 brothers, and each brother has 2 brothers and 4 sisters.*

*This can be done mathematically S = the number of sisters and B = the number of brothers:*
*S - 1 = B*
*2(B - 1) = S*

*Solving for S gives you 4 and plugging that in to B - 1 = B gives you a B of 3.*

### 77. _**The Car Thieves**_

*We know whoever stole the Jaguar was telling the truth. Both Andy and Liam say they did not steal the Jaguar, so it must have been Jack who stole it.*

*That means that Jack was telling the truth which means that Liam stole the Mercedes. That leaves Andy with the Bentley.*

### 78. _**Rich and Poor**_

*Fred and Lisa are both rich*

*If Fred is telling the truth, then Lisa is poor and telling the truth as well. If this is the case, then Fred would be rich and lying.*

*Similarly, if Lisa is telling the truth.*

*They must therefore both be lying and are rich.*

79. **<u>Hour Glasses</u>**

*At 0 minutes:*
*start both hourglasses at the same time.*
*At 4 minutes:*
*4 minutes hourglass runs out and flip it. 7 minutes hourglass is left with 3 minutes.*
*At 7 minutes:*
*4 minutes hourglass is left with 1 minute. 7 minutes hourglass runs out and flip it.*
*At 8 minutes:*
*4 minutes hourglass runs out and 7 is filled with 6 minutes. Pour sand from 7 minutes hourglass to 4 minutes so that the 4 minutes hour glass becomes full. Now 7 minutes hourglass is left with 1 minute*
*At 9 minutes:*
*7 minutes hourglass becomes empty.*

*Therefore, we have measured 9 minutes.*

80. **<u>The Traveler</u>**

*As he arrived home 10 minutes early it means that his wife saved 5 minutes of each way of the trip. She must have picked him up at 4.55pm.*

*As he started walking at 4pm he must have walked for 55 minutes*

## 81. **_The Perilous Room_**

You ask one of the guards what the other guard would say was the safe route out and do the opposite.

If the guard you ask tells the truth then he will say what the lying guard would say. Therefore, you will do the opposite of that.

If the guard you ask is the lying guard then he will lie about what the truthful guard will say, so again you will do the opposite of what he says.

## 82. **_A Pet Pigeon_**

The cyclists must travel 36 miles and travel at a joint speed of 12mph. They will therefore take 3 hours to reach their meeting point.

The pigeon travels at 18mph and will therefore travel 54 miles.

## 83. **_The Zookeeper_**

The order they were fed was;
Monkeys
Bears
Giraffes
Zebras
Lions

## 84. **_Burglar Bill_**

The value to weight ratios are

Diamond - £3.28/kg
Sapphire - £3.27/kg
Rubies - £3kg

Therefore, it is logical for Bill to fill his bag with the most value per Kg.

The 5 diamonds would weigh 35kg and be worth £115. This leaves room for 17kg in the bag.

1 sapphire would weigh 11 kg and be worth £36.

This leaves 6kg remaining in the bag which will accommodate 2 rubies which are worth £20.

The total value of the haul is therefore £171

85. **_A Bag of Spuds_**
The bag weighs 10lb which is 50/5

86. **_The Tourists_**
There are 5 men, 20 women and 10 children.

If x = the number of men
Then x + 2x + 4x = 35
7x = 35
X = 5

87. **_The Legacy_**
Ian received $240 and David $760.

*If 80 (one third of 240) is taken from 190 (one quarter of 760) then the remainder is 110.*

### 88. **Jack and Jen**
*Jack's age is 7 and Jen's is 13*

### 89. **Bill's Painters**
*One painter can do one room in two hours. Therefore, in six hours he could do three rooms.*

*To do 18 rooms will take 6 painters.*

### 90. **A Number**
*27*

### 91. **Harrod's**
*If we add all the items together we get 83 + 77 + 62 + 95 = 317 items.*

*As these were shared among 100 women this means that a minimum of 17 women must have had all four items.*

### 92. **Ann's Age**
*Ann's age is 32, her brother's 34, her sister's 38 and her mother 52*

### 93. **_The Mathematician_**

The mathematician put a small amount of fencing around his legs so that he was standing in the middle and declared himself to be on the outside.

### 94. **_Clock Face_**

It isn't zero degrees.

At quarter past the minute hand will be on the three so it will be at 90 degrees.

However, the hour hand will be one quarter of the way between 3 and 4. Therefore the difference will be;

1/4 x 1/12 x 360 degrees = 7.5 degrees

### 95. **_The Windy Dog_**

With the wind the dog averages 20mph and against the wind it averages 15mph. Therefore, the wind speed is 2.5mph and without the wind the dog would average 17.5mph

A mile would take 60/17.5 minutes which is 3 3/7 minutes.

### 96. **_Pill Taking_**

One pill is taken at 6am and another at 10pm. The question is to find two evenly spaced times within the 16 hours to take the remaining two pills.

*The answer is 5 hours 20 minutes between pills. This means;*
*First pill – 6am*
*Second pill – 11:20am*
*Third pill – 4:40pm*
*Fourth pill – 10pm*

## 97. *Friends Age*

*The answer is 49*

*As we are not counting Saturdays and Sundays there are only 5 days in each of their weeks - there are of course 7 days in each week. So, if we divide the 35 by the 5 days and then multiply by the 7 days we have the answer 49*

## 98. *A Child*

*In six years time Ann will be 27. If she is 5 times the age of her child then the child will be 5.4 years old, or 5 years and 146 days.*

*Therefore 6 years prior the child had not yet been born. Given an average pregnancy of 280 days the mother is 61 days into her pregnancy.*

*As six years prior there were 219 days to go before the child's birth the child's age is – 219 days.*

## 99. **Mince Pies**

*The first customer buys 3/4 which leaves 1/4 .*

*The second customer takes 1/8 + 7 which leaves 9.*

*Therefore 1/8x = 7 + 9 = 16*

*x = 16 x 8 = 128 mince pies*

## 100. **Sugar and Spice**

*The intuitive answer is boys but if you said that you would be wrong.*

*If we imagine two sibling families we can get BB, BG, GB or GG.*

*The four boys have a total of two sisters as do the four girls.*

*If we take three sibling families we get BBB, BBG, BGB, GBB, GGB, GBG, GGB and GGG. The 12 boys have a total of 12 sisters as do the girls.*

*The answer is that they both have the same number of sisters.*

## 101. **A Long Piece of String**

*Surprisingly the string would be hovering about 1.6m above the earth.*

*The circumference is 2πr. If you divide 40,000,000 and 40,000,010 by π then you will get the diameter. If you divide the diameter of the two numbers by 2 you will* get the increase in radius as a result of the increase of 10m in the circumference.

## 102. **_The Necktie Paradox_**

Both men don't have an advantage. If we take the situation of the first man with assumed tie values;

| Price of tie | Price of 2nd man's tie | Gain/loss |
|---|---|---|
| $20 | $20 | 0 |
| $20 | $40 | $40 gain |
| $40 | $20 | $40 loss |
| $40 | $40 | 0 |

The first man has a 50% chance of no gain and a 25% each of a gain or loss, similarly for the second man.

Therefore, neither man has an advantage

## 103. **_Pool Party Coke_**

If you place both cans in the pool the diet coke will float but the regular coke will sink. A regular coke sinks because it has sugar which makes the density heavier than water

## 104. **_Solve the Sum_**

C could be 0 or 5 as they are the only digits to make the final column correct. If it was 0 that would make the sum 000 which is not possible as the digits are different.

*Therefore, C = 5.*

*The sum is therefore 555 and 3(A + B + C) = 555. If we divide both sides by three we get 185.*

*S o A = 1, B = 8 and C = 5*

### 105. **House Hunting**

*There are 45 years left.*

### 106. **Weights**

*You will need weights of 1lb, 3lbs, 9lbs and 17lbs. Any weight up to 30lbs can be made using these weights.*

### 107. **The Marksman**

*The first chamber he fired was one of four empty chambers. As the bullets were placed into consecutive chambers one of those is followed by a bullet and three by an empty chamber.*

*If the chamber just fired was the one next to the bullets, a 1 in 4 chance, then it will fire a bullet if the chamber is not spun.*

*If the chamber is spun there are 2 out of 6 chambers with a bullet so the odds are 1 in 3.*

*The odds are greater on firing a bullet if he spins the chamber.*

### 108. ***St Ives***

*Just one, me.*

### 109. ***In the Darkness***

*Auntie Jane was blind and was reading a braille book*

### 110. ***Poultry Puzzle***

*The price of a chicken was $2.00, for a duck $4.00, and for a goose $5.00.*

# EVIL ANSWERS

### 111. _**The Bridge**_

Yes, they can all cross within 15 minutes. The trick is to have the two slowest people crossing together.

Time

2 mins       _Andy and Betty cross_

3 mins       _Andy returns with the torch_

11 mins      _Chris and Diane cross_

13 mins      _Betty returns with the torch_

15 mins      _Andy and Betty cross_

### 112. _**The Missing Dollar**_

This is a case of misdirection. The guests did indeed pay $9 each once the bellhop had given then $1 each. If we then take the $2 he kept off that we get to $25 which was the revised cost of the room.

We need to take the $2 off the $27 to get to $25 rather than add it on and hope to get to $30.

### 113. _**Loving and Giving**_

The first letters of the name are days of the week. The fifth one is Frank, for Friday

## 114. **_The Census_**

The simplest solution is to go through what the number could be that multiplied together up to 72 and what they add up to. These are:

1, 1 and 72 = 74

1, 2 and 36 = 39

1, 3 and 24 = 28

1, 4 and 18 = 23

1, 6 and 12 = 19

1, 8 and 9 = 18

2, 2 and 18 = 22

2, 3 and 12 = 17

2, 4 and 9 = 15

2, 6 and 6 = 14

3, 3 and 8 = 14

3, 4 and 6 = 13

Now we know that this was not sufficient information for the census taker. That means that the number on the gate must have been 14 as there are two sets of ages which add up to 72.

However, when the women said she was going to see her eldest child that meant the children's ages were 3, 3 and 8 as that is the combination of ages with an eldest child.

## 115. _**The Monty Hall Problem**_

_Rather counterintuitively your chances if you switch are 2/3 of winning the Ferrari and 1/3 if you don't._

_The trick is in the fact that the host knew where the car was. You pick a door to start with and your chance of winning is 1/3, which means that there is a $2/3^{rd}$ chance the car is behind one of the other two doors._

_If the host then eliminates a door with nothing behind it doesn't alter the odds of 2/3rds. It just means that there is only one door to choose rather than two with a 2/3rds probability._

_If you are unconvinced consider a case with 1,000 doors. You choose door 1 then the host eliminates 998 doors with nothing behind and gives you a choice. Which would you choose?_

## 116. _**Camels and Bananas**_

_What you need to do is to create a drop point part of the way there. The first drop point needs to be 200 miles towards your destination._

_To take all 3,000 bananas will involve two trips to the 200 mile drop point and back and a final one way trip. This will make 1,000 miles traveled and 1,000 bananas eaten leaving 2,000._

*The next stop is a further 334 miles towards the final destination. This will involve one trip there and back and one final trip with the final 1,000 bananas. The total mileage in this part is 1,002 and will leave 998 bananas for the final part of the trip.*

*The first and second trip went 534 miles leaving 466 miles left to go. The camel will eat a further 466 bananas and deliver 998 – 466 = 532 at the destination*

## 117. *Card Puzzle*

*Whether there is a vowel or a consonant on the other side of the third card with the number 2 makes no difference.*

*The statement "every card with a vowel on one side has an even number on its opposite side" can only be shown to be false if there is an odd number on the opposite site of the first card showing an E and/or a vowel on the opposite side of the fourth card showing a 3*

## 118. *Cheryl's Birthday*

*This is solved by a process of elimination.*

*Remember, Albert is told either May, June, July or August.*
*Bernard is told either 14, 15, 16, 17, 18 or 19*

*Let's go through it line by line.*

*(Line 1) "Albert: I don't know when Cheryl's birthday is, but I know that Bernard doesn't know too".*
*The only way Bernard would know the date with a single number would be if it were the 18th or 19th as these only appear once, May 18th and June 19th.*
*For Albert to be certain that Bernard didn't know must mean that May and June couldn't be the months, as Bernard would have done if the date he had been given were the 18th or 19th.*

*(Line 2) "Bernard: Then I know when Cheryl's birthday is."*
*Bernard has deduced that Albert has either August or July. If he knows the full date, he must have been told 15, 16 or 17, since if he had been told 14 he would be none the wiser about whether the month was August or July. Each of 15, 16 and 17 only refers to one specific month, but 14 could be either month.*

*Line 3) Albert: "Then I also know when Cheryl's birthday is."*

*Albert has therefore deduced that the possible dates are July 16, Aug 15 and Aug 17. For him to now know, he must have been told July. Since if he had been told August, he would not know which date for certain is the birthday.*

*The answer, therefore is July 16.*

## 119. **Elephants**
*The trick is to add an imaginary elephant to the herd so that it totals 16.*

*The first son therefore gets ½ the herd which is 8. The second son then gets ¾ of the remaining elephants which is 6 and the third son gets ½ of the 2 left which is 1.*

*That leaves 1 elephant which is our imaginary elephant, so none are left behind and the proportions in the will are satisfied.*

### 120. **Two Boats**
*i) When they cross the first time they have travelled a combined distance of one river width.*

*ii) When they cross the second time they have travelled a combined distance of three rivers width.*

*iii) On the second meeting they had travelled three times as far as at the first meeting.*

*iv) As boat A had travelled 720 yards at the first meeting it has travelled 2,160 yards at the second meeting.*

*v) As boat A was 400 yards into its return trip that makes the rivers width 1,760 yards.*

### 121. **A Light Bulb**
*You flick the switch A on and leave it for 10 minutes. Then you switch this off and flick switch B on and open the door.*
*If the light is on, then it is switch B. If the bulb is hot it is switch A. If neither of these apply, then it is switch C.*

### 122. **The True Statement**

*Only one statement in the list can be true as they are mutually exclusive. That would imply that only one statement can be true and nine are false.*

*Therefore, statement nine that nine statements are false is the true one.*

### 123. _A Railway Journey_
*512.*

*Station 10 is only visited once as he turns around there so he can only take a photo then.*

*The other 9 he can take on the outward or return trip. Therefore, the number of combinations is:*

*2x2x2x2x2x2x2x2x2 = 512*

### 124. _Dates_
*The 17th of June 2345*

*(17/6/2345)*

### 125. _Bank Account_
*A bit of a trick question as your account was overdrawn by £100. Therefore, after the transaction the account was;*

*(-100) x 2 = -200*

*The amount of money has doubled, though it is a negative number.*

### 126. _How Old_

*Alex is 64 and Tim is 48. When Alex was 48 Tim*
*was 32, which is half Alex's age now*

## 127. Which Letter

*If you can unscramble your brain you will find the*
*answer is the latter H*

## 128. Socks

*The chances of pulling out a pair of black socks is zero.*
*For him to half a ½ chance of pulling out a pair of*
*white socks there must be 3 white and 1 black in the*
*drawer.*

## 129. Bags of Money

*The money is put into the bags as follows: $1, 2 ,4, 8,*
*16, 32, 64, 128, 256 and 489.*

*The first nine are a geometric progression and the sum*
*of these are subtracted from $1,000 to get the last*
*number.*

## 130. A Will

*We know the wives received;*
*Catherine - $122*
*Jane - $132*
*Mary - $142*

*That leaves $604 to be distributed among the*
*husbands. This is done by;*

*John Smith receiving the same as his wife Catherine -*
*$122*

Henry Jones receives half as much again as his wife Jane - $198

Tom White receives twice as much as his wife Mary - $284

That adds up to the $604 remaining in the will

### 131. <u>Cubes and Squares</u>

$10^2 - 6^2 = 100 - 36 = 64 = 4^3$

$10^3 - 6^3 = 1,000 - 216 = 784 = 28^2$

### 132. <u>The Olympics</u>

FirsT = GolD, SeconD = SilveR therefore ThirD = BronzE

So the answer is BE

### 133. <u>Vexillogy</u>

Australia. The number refers to the number of stars on the national flag.

### 134. <u>The Dodgy Clock</u>

We know for every 60 minutes the clock shows 56 minutes, so 56 minutes on the clock is an hour

By 15:52 the clock will be 952 minutes beyond midnight. If you divide this by 56 you will get 17 which is the actual hours.

If you then add on the 90 minutes that have elapsed since the clock stopped, you get 18 hours 30 minutes.

*The time is therefore 18:30.*

## 135. <u>The Shoelace</u>

*The easiest way to think about this is two people traveling the same journey. One stops before the travellator to tie their shoe laces and one gets on it and then ties their shoe laces.*

*The person who ties their shoe laces on the solid ground will never catch up.*

## 136. <u>Triples</u>

*The answer is "You are great"*

*The numbers are groups of three and the addition of these numbers correspond to the number a letter is in the alphabet. A = 1, B = 2 etc*

## 137. <u>Plane Seating</u>

*The answer is he has a 50% chance of sitting in his proper seat.*

*There are two possibilities;*

*If any of the first 99 sit in Jane's seat then Jack will get his seat.*

*If any of the first 99 sit in Jack's seat then he won't get his seat.*

## 138. *The Twelve Days of Christmas*

The number of gifts are;

Partridges: 1 × 12 = 12
Doves: 2 × 11 = 22
Hens 3 × 10 = 30
Calling birds: 4 × 9 = 36
Golden rings: 5 × 8 = 40
Geese: 6 × 7 = 42
Swans: 7 × 6 = 42
Maids: 8 × 5 = 40
Ladies: 9 × 4 = 36
Lords: 10 × 3 = 30
Pipers: 11 × 2 = 22
Drummers: 12 × 1 = 12

Total = 364

The gifts will have run out by the following Christmas Day

## 139. *An Athletic Mind*

They are the Olympian running distances for athletics divided by 100.

## 140. *Animal Encyclopedia*

The trick here is to imagine the two books on the shelf. Let's start with the first volume. If you think about it Aardvark will be on the first page which will be on the right side of the spine as it sits on the shelf.

Similarly, Zebra will be on the left of the spine of the second volume.

*The difference between the bookmarks will therefore be 2 covers of 2mm. The answer to the nearest centimetre is 0*

## 141. <u>The Queen of Hearts</u>

*The puzzle looks impenetrable but the knaves all disagree so only one can be telling the truth.*

*If only one is telling the truth, then four are lying so four ate the tarts.*

*If all 5 were lying the Knave 5 would be telling the truth which is self-contradictory.*

*Therefore, Knave 4 is telling the truth.*

## 142. <u>Football Scam</u>

*Unfortunately, Jane's early retirement is delayed because it is a scam.*

*If there were an equal probability of a win, lose or draw then 7 correct predictions would be 1 in 2,187 which is impressive.*

*However, the correct prediction is achieved because of the amount of emails the scammer sent out.*

*Therefore, if the scammer sent out 1,000,000 emails he would make the seven correct consecutive predictions in 457 cases on average.*

*The scammer will then send out the first email predicting a win, lose or draw to a third each of his audience. Those who received the correct forecast will then receive the second email predicting a win, lose or draw and so on.*

*Eventually the relatively small number who happened to receive the seven correct answers will then receive the claim for £1,000.*

### 143. <u>The St Petersburg Paradox</u>
*The answer is yes.*

*Half the time tails comes up first and you will win $1. A quarter of the time it comes up second toss and you will win $2, and so on.*

*The amount you can win will get bigger as the odds of winning it get smaller.*

*The winnings will be;*
*(1/2 x $1) + (1/4 x $2) + (1/8 x $4) + (1/16 x $8) ...*

*This equates to 50c + 50c + 50c + 50c ad infinitum. So, your expected winnings are infinite!*

### 144. <u>Four Fours</u>
$0 = 4 \div 4 \times (4 - 4)$
$1 = 4 \div 4 + (4 - 4)$
$2 = (4 \div 4) + (4 \div 4)$
$3 = (4 \times 4 - 4) \div 4$
$4 = 4 \times (4-4) + 4$
$5 = (4 \times 4 + 4) \div 4$
$6 = (4 + 4) \div 4 + 4$

$7 = 4 + 4 - (4 \div 4)$

$8 = (4 \div 4) \times 4 + 4$

$9 = (4 \div 4) + 4 + 4$

$10 = 4 \div \sqrt{4}) + (4 \times \sqrt{4})$

$11 = (4! \times \sqrt{4} - 4) \div 4$

$12 = 4 \times (4 - 4 \div 4)$

$13 = (4! \times \sqrt{4} + 4) \div 4$

$14 = (4 \times 4) - (4 \div \sqrt{4})$

$15 = 4 \times 4 - (4 \div 4)$

$16 = 4 \times 4 + (4 - 4)$

$17 = 4 \times 4 + (4 \div 4)$

$18 = 4 \times 4 + (4 - \sqrt{4})$

$19 = 4! - 4 - (4 \div 4)$

$20 = 4 \times (4 + 4 \div 4)$

$21 = 4! - 4 + (4 \div 4)$

$22 = 4! \div 4 + (4 \times 4)$

$23 = (4! \times 4 - 4) \div 4$

$24 = 4 \times 4 + 4 + 4$

$25 = (4! \times 4 + 4) \div 4$

$4!$ (factorial) $= 4 \times 3 \times 2 \times 1 = 24$

## 145. <u>Sixteen Fours</u>

$444 + 444 + 44 + 44 + 4 + 4 + 4 + 4 + 4 + 4 = 1,000$

## 146. <u>A Peculiar Liar</u>

What we know is that Zac tells the truth on one day of the week.

If the statement on day 1 is untrue, this means that he tells the truth on Monday or Tuesday. If the statement *on day 3 is untrue, this means that he tells the truth on Wednesday or Friday. Since Zac tells the truth on only one day, these statements cannot both be untrue. So, exactly one of these statements must be true, and the statement on day 2 must be untrue.*

*Assume that the statement on day 1 is true. Then the statement on day 3 must be untrue, from which follows that Zac tells the truth on Wednesday or Friday. So, day 1 is a Wednesday or a Friday. Therefore, day 2 is a Thursday or a Saturday. However, this would imply that the statement on day 2 is true, which is impossible. From this we can conclude that the statement on day 1 must be untrue.*

*This means that Zac told the truth on day 3 and that this day is a Monday or a Tuesday. So day 2 is a Sunday or a Monday. Because the statement on day 2 must be untrue, we can conclude that day 2 is a Monday.*

*So, day 3 is a Tuesday. Therefore, the day on which Zac tells the truth is Tuesday.*

## 147. <u>Drugs Test</u>

*Despite the test being 99% accurate, if an individual from 1,000 tests positive, it is more likely that they do not use the drug than that they do.*

*This surprising result arises because the number of non-users is very large compared to the number of* users. To use concrete numbers, if 1000 individuals are tested and assume 0.5% are drug users. There are expected to be 995 non-users and 5 users. From the 995 non-users, false positives are expected.

From the 5 users, true positives are expected. Out of 15 positive results, only 5, 33%, are genuine.

### 148. _A Sound Riddle_
Each word rhymes with the number it corresponds with. i.e. gun with one, shoe with two etc

### 149. _Einstein's Puzzle_
The solution is that the person in house 4 owns the fish. The situation looks like this in order of color, country, drink, smoke and pet.

House 1: yellow, Norwegian, water, dunhill, cats
House 2: blue, Dane, tea, blend, horse
House 3: red, British, milk, pall mall, birds
House 4: green, German, coffee, prince, fish
House 5: white, Swedish, beer, bluemaster, dogs

### 150. _The Prisoner's Trees_
The trick is that by passing the question when they don't know the answer passes information between them.

Day 1; When James is asked if there are 18 or 20 trees he could only give an answer if he could see 19 or 20 trees. So, he must pass.

*This tells Carly that James can only see 18 trees at most.*

*Similarly, when Carly is asked the question if she could only see 0 or 1 tree then she could conclude that there were 18 trees. However, as she can see 8 she must pass.*

*This tells James that Carly must be able to see at least 2 trees.*

*Day 2; They can build on this information to inform them when they are asked the question on day 2.*

*If James could see 17 or 18 trees he would be able to answer 20 trees as Carly can see at least 2. However, as he can see 12 he has to pass again.*

*This tells Carly that James can see at most 16 trees.*

*Similarly, when Carly is asked if she could see 2 or 3 trees she would know the total was 18 as James can only see 16 at most. However, she must pass.*

*This tells James that Carly must be able to see at least 4 trees.*

*Day 3; If James could see 15 or 16 trees he could conclude, Carly seeing at least 4, that 20 trees was the answer. He must pass again.*

*This again tells Carly that James must be seeing at least 14 trees.*

*Similarly, if Carly saw 4 or 5 trees she could conclude with James seeing at most 14 that 18 was the answer. As she sees 8 she must pass again.*

*That tells James Carly must have seen at least 6 trees.*

*Day 4; If James sees 13 or 14 trees he can conclude there are 20 trees. As he sees 12 he must pass.*

*Carly realises that James can see at most 12 trees.*

*If Carly saw 6 or 7 trees, then she could conclude that 18 was the answer. She sees 8 so passes.*

*James realises that Carly must be able to see at least 8 trees.*

*Day 5; As James can see 12 trees and knows that Carly can see 8 he can exclude 18 as the answer which only leaves 20 as the total number of trees.*

*James answers 20 and they are both set free!*

**Well done if you got that. You are an expert logician.**

Printed in Great
Britain
by Amazon